World Healing World Peace

Poetry

2014

Volume I

inner child press, ltd.

Credits

Compilation

Janet P. Caldwell

Foreword

Fahredin Shehu

Preface

William S. Peters, Sr.

a few Words

Dr. hülya n. yilmaz
Dr. Peter C. Rogers

Cover Graphics

Chyna Blue
edifyin' graphix

General Information

World Healing ~ World Peace Volume I
Inner Child Press, ltd.

1st Edition : 2014

Publisher Information

1st Edition : Inner Child Press :
intouch@innerchildpress.com
www.innerchildpress.com

ISBN-13 : 978-0615996073 (Inner Child Press, Ltd.)

ISBN-10 : 0615996078

$ 16.95

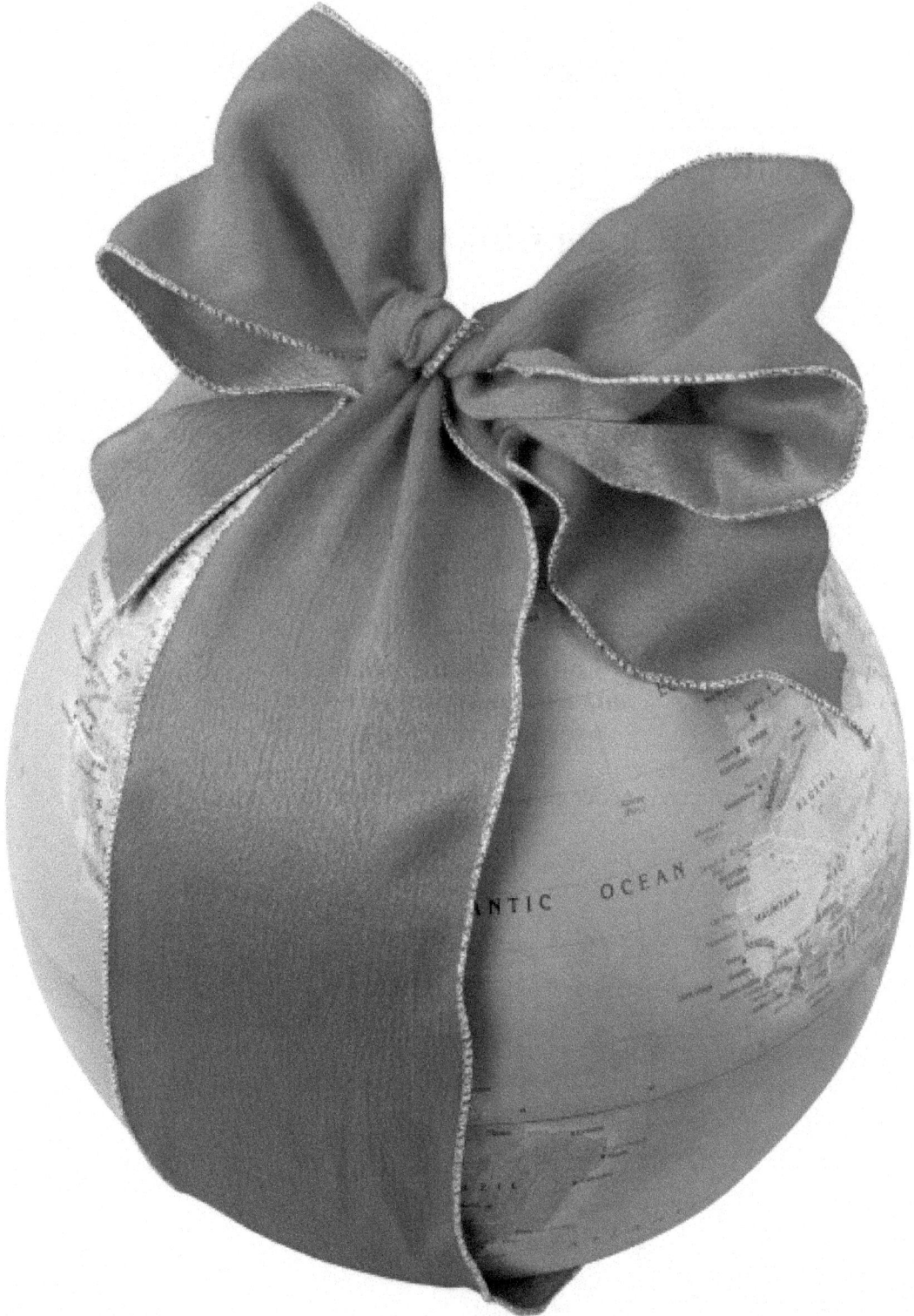

Dedication

This offering is dedicated to Humanity

. . . and it's resurrection.

my Sun is Orange

my morning Sun is orange
The yellow is stained
with the Blood of my People
for that is what we
are reminded of
each day

when it rises from the East
to greet the world
i see my world
clearly

we once lived with a hope
that the atrocities of Hate
War
and indifference
would go away
but it did not

my hope has been misplaced
somewhere
and i can not remember
where i have set it down

it might have been that day
i lost my arm
or that day
when my Father was jailed
or that day
when my Sister was killed
she was only 3

no, i think i lost my hope
the day
my Mother no longer cried

her eyes have been dry
for many a year now
and somehow
by some grace
she still has enough love in her

to hug me
once in a while
through that pained smile
that still adorns her face
just so she won't completely break

there is a noise i hear
it is a loud silence
that stays with me
through my callousness
for the gunfire
and the bombs
and the screams
i can not hear them

they have long ago
assaulted and killed
the dreams of my Family
my village
my people
and it is now working on
Humanity

where is the sanity
in this methodology
to be found

every day is "Ground Zero"
where i live
every where i look
i see Ground Zeros
and we have lost count
of those who
are no more
because of what you call War

but you and i
never had a dispute
that i know of
If so, please tell me what i did wrong
to cause you harm
that you should exact such wretchedness
upon me
and others like me

i know not of the Politics
of it all.
i have never met a Politician
are they so different
than we the people ?

if it's Oil
i give it to you
if it's right
take it freely
i will not raise nor put my hand
against that
of my Father's children

there was a time
when all i thought of
was simply
finding Joy in my life
i have since given up that quest
for i see far too much
of that other stuff
which deserves not a name

my Sun is no longer Yellow
but i do pray my Brother
that yours is

my Sun is Orange

This is dedicated to all the Villages, Peoples across our Globe who must endure the
Politics and Sickness of War.

Foreword

to the Members of One Body

"Human beings are all members of one body. They are created from the same essence. When one member is in pain, The others cannot rest. If you do not care about the pain of others, You do not deserve to be called a human being."

Mosleh al-Din Saadi Shirazi
13th century Persian poet, from Shiraz

~ * ~

There are myriads of words Men had had uttered throughout its historical life journey leaving the rich legacy of conscience, endeavor, struggle to remain the essence of Unique and Uniqueness of Creation. The Word has killed Men and the Word is able to cure Men. The Word has burned many hearts and many evil hearts has burned the Word in Men's History. Today as in every age again there are some people unable to remain passive bystanders for the wounds of the world.

This world as it was cursed by us, Men alone, to suffer in continuation of her existence. At least what they may do is screaming to tell the Truth, and the Truth is that the World today needs the Healing.

We have to always be amazed with the power of some individuals to bring together those very Human who scream to say the Truth, the Truth of their Capacity, the Truth of their Creativity, the Truth of their Justice and the Truth of their Human Potentials in an "Understandable Language", that goes beyond simplicity, people who are set alone, themselves alone, to create a beautiful Word as manner of healing themselves, healing others and the World, who are scarifying their time, their creativity and their entire being.

This Anthology typically represents the Beauty created with sacrifice…the palette of colors and the nuances, sounds and the grandeur of pain, the hollow voices that comes from eternity going through the prism of nowadays turbulences, walking from country to country from continent to another to gather in one spot, in one aim as an arrow to hit the target of contemporary Men's consciousness.

The reader of these lines shall be delighted to read the elements of the others' beings the quintessence of these incredible Poets and Poetesses, without wanting to distinguish names since for me there is no the best Poets, there is always the best time and the best mood to have the splendor and joy in absorbing ones word, when the one is in tune with the being, with the breath, and with the momentum. They do as they want to say to us: "We have tamed our wildness, come and join us, come and rejoice, for Peace shall belong to all it is a right not a privilege."

I'm indeed much honored to be the one who writes the open Word for this Anthology and express the gratitude to William S. Peters, Sr. who made it possible for me possible to be among these incredible words created by these incredible Humans, and my gratitude reaches the whiteness of the clouds. Only those who are able to build bridges among nations, religious background, ethnicities and genders; are able to understand the importance of this Noble effort. This is indeed a noble endeavor!!!

Thank you Inner Child Press

Fahredin Shehu

March, 2014
Prishtina Kosovo

Fahredin Shehu

Born in Rahovec, South East of Kosova, in 1972. graduated at Prishtina University, Oriental Studies.

Actively works on Calligraphy discovering new mediums and techniques for this specific for of plastic art.

Certified expert in Andragogy/ Capacity Building, Training delivery, Coaching and Mentoring, Facilitating etc.

In last ten years he operated as Independent Scientific Researcher in the field of World Spiritual Heritage and Sacral Esthetics.

Preface

It is not just because i have children and i have concerns for their safety and welfare, but the fact of the matter is you may have children too. Actually we are all children of this wonder filled Creation who inhabit this Awe Inspiring Planet we call Earth.

When i think in terms of World Healing ~ World Peace, like most of us there is much about us that needs our attention, adjustment and resolution. I like most of us could sit and complain the remainder of our lives away about all that is wrong. The predominant aspect of what i would like to ultimately transfer in the way of energy to every on i can, is that we have the ability to effectuate the changes we desire. We have the power to reconcile our existence to that of our Dreams of Utopia. "Our World" is inherently one of abundance and i believe there is enough for all of us to coexist in a peaceful, loving manner. For too long we have allowed the few to control the many. This would include most of our institutions from Religion, Politics, Education, Business, Food, Medicine, Media and Finance.

Our desires for "Things" along with the rampant Greed we witness has gone just about as far as we should allow. However, in order to make the much needed equitable adjustments for parity, we must first examine and correct the archaic consciousness' we hold to unwittingly. The depth of our indoctrination fed to us by the controlling class is a tangled web filled with deceits and ulterior motives and agendas that do not serve the masses of people who have need for such basic things as Drinking Water, Food, Medical Attention and the lack of War and Strife.

Many may ask, "How can we achieve this end?" . . . well, i have always been told that "every journey begins with the first step". Many have already taken that initial step, while some are waiting for the right motivation.

We have chosen the medium of Poetry and Prose to relay our messages from around the world. In this our second effort to evoke a higher level of participatory consciousness we hope that you find the words that moves you to care enough to be moved to a certifiable action that contributes to the good of us all.

Our aspiration here with this effort of World Healing ~ World Peace Poetry 2014, is not only to just produce a book, but to distribute the book and get it into the hands of our World's Policymakers. We have a campaign to deliver copies to every member Country of the United Nations as well as every voting member of The United States Congress. we can not do this alone. There is a Fund Raising Campaig still active to achieve this goal. If you can not contribute, please do take the time to share the message!

Funding Campaign
http://www.gofundme.com/3gvqks

The Video
http://www.youtube.com/watch?v=0MMttNrig4I

World Healing ~ World Peace
Poetry 2014
www.worldhealingworldpeacepoetry.com

World Healing ~ World Peace Now

William S. Peters, Sr.

Inner Child Enterprises, ltd.
www.iaminnerchild.com

Table of Contents

Poetry

Table of Contents . . . *continued*

*T*able of *C*ontents . . . *continued*

*E*pilogue   113

www.worldhealingworldpeacepoetry.com

World Healing World Peace

Poetry

2014

Volume I

inner child press, ltd.

One word at a time, we as writers, deciphered our affect towards change for the basic principles of humanity. Through this collaborative effort, the initiative moves into the hands of our leaders, the diplomats of our freedoms, well-being, and peace. Whether they choose to page beyond the cover, and appreciate a literate world for change is now up to them.

Diane Sismour

Fahredin Shehu is a World Class Poet and Ambassador for Humanity. Born in Rahovec, South East of Kosova, in 1972. Graduated at Prishtina University, Oriental Studies.

His works have been translated into English, French, Italian, Spanish, Serbian, Croatian, Bosnian, Macedonian, Roma, Swedish, Turkish, Arabic, Hebrew, Romanian, Persian, Mongolian, Chinese.

He is the Ambassador of Poets to Albania by Poetas del Mundo, Santiago de Chile, Member of World Poets Association, Kosovo Pen Center.

http://www.innerchildpress.com/fahredin-shehu.php

Green Muffin Hills

(I'm the ashes beneath your holly feet my Miriai)

Blood cells turned blue…
a mass of blue kelp floats,
somewhere amidst nine layers of fog;
You see no one except the "I".

You see…there's no one encroached ever,
the valleys of green muffin hills resembling,
Darjeeling fields with the white clouds just near the leafs

Sprinkled pearls of dew… in them alloyed rhizoid bacteria
fertilizing the images of someone supposed to be Spiritual Something
but where?- where is the one who felt down in despair for the Men lost the idea for

the Magic of something called Love, and the Hexes of Creativity beyond visible forms
and shapes disperses, and colors, and nuances, and sound, and vibrations, and feelings,
and destinations…
and destinations…
and destinations…

…and the tree that laments the death of lianas embracing its marvelous body as old as
Holy Scriptures, those who evaporate the smell of Nard and keep between its pages the
wreaths of Myrrh…oh Mother Miriai: "I'm the ashes beneath your holly feet when you
swear in Certitude": **In my forehead there's a testimony, the Angel of the Right
Shoulder and the Angel of my Left…are witness what my Womb bears**: for others
are unable to see what you saw, Miriai. No, there were never neither they would ever be
able to see, what you saw:- what I saw…what I saw…what I saw…what I saw…what I…

2

James Dooney

James is a 39 year old poet from Australia, currently teaching English in Korea. He loves to write. He is on numerous Facebook and Linkedin poetry groups and he hopes to see some of you there also !!! he also love music, Kimchi and would love to pursue writing as a serious career soon enough.

My thoughts on the subject of change...

My thoughts
on a little matter
important to us all
here we go ..

We can bond creation
with evolution
for if we do
we can bring about
a revolution.

At the same time
We can grant emancipation
to our wondrous global nation
and bring about a daring
glaring
and indeed blaring
new sensation.

It is also true that
We can be
our own rocket
We can blow
our own socket
and that we need'nt-all-day
sit within our pocket.

For If we heed the call
we can hear it all
so lets lay it all out
lets roll our ball

But in rolling your ball
please pay attention
for that thing ahead
that bright shining light
sure ain't always Mr Right.

Yet on the left
lies a new cleft
keying a sound
unbereft

telling us too..

Love all things
preferably for free
for in doing so
you free your mind
and this should always be

At least somewhat,
as we wont hit it all the time but its worth trying to be..
a central target
a direction
and an end point in our range.
Something that we can achieve
upon the road
we travel
to change.

I am sure
I am not
the only one
with such
throbbing
mobbing
and sometimes mentally blobbing
thoughts..

Tony Henninger

I came from Germany to the U.S. at the age of 12. I live in Texas and love music and poetry. I am an avid reader and student, trying to enlighten myself and others to make this world a better place. I am a strong believer in the power of love.

http://www.innerchildpress.com/tony-henninger.php

Let Love And Peace Reign

When will there be enough death
before wars will come to an end?
When will enough children have died
before hearts can begin to mend?

If only my words could stop
the bombs from falling.
If only my tears could stop
the guns from firing.
If only my song could make
the whole world sing.
If only my heart and soul
enough love could bring.

Maybe if I shouted louder?
Maybe if I cried harder?
Maybe if I sacrificed all of me?
Maybe if I loved everyone equally?

But, I know, I can't do it alone.
I need everyone to look inside.
Open your hands and drop the stone.
Hold my hand and stand by my side.
Sing with me a song of peace,
love, compassion, and kindness.
Let's stop all the sadness.
Let's stop all the madness.

If we want to live,
we all have to give.
So, I say to you, my friends,
join me in this affirmation:
To love each other unconditionally.
To bring about change to Humanity.
For we all have the same dream.
We live under the same sun.
Forever let Love and Peace reign.
Let our hearts become One.
AMEN!

Janet Renee Cryer

I owe the Lord all the glory and power whispering messages in my ear. Having worn many belts in my life, mom, wife, lover, I have been blessed and cursed with many experiences. One will live through my battle with manic depression, helping other, loving, and love lost reading my works.

Walls Of Shells

The shells of the seas become stronger,
Each one piled on top of the other,
The sands of time filling in the spaces,
Cementing and strengthening the bond,
Once the walls are put together,
One sees a dark spot,
The spot growing,
It weakened the stability,
So the bond makers need to look to another to repair,
Yet, one couldn't see past the flaw,
It grew to unbearable tension that prevented the bond maker to continue building,
So the walls start to fall,
Coming and going,
Making promises that a foundation would still be built,
The bond makers continue the mirage until it fails,
Or did it ?
One continuing to fill the holes with sand,
Didn't realize the strength brought to the bond,
Though it wasn't the strength of two that became one,
It was the personal strength of a foundation built,
Yet, the waves come crashing,
Sands start falling,
She can't see her strength was and has always been stronger,
Just seeing the pain of solitary building,
So while the assistant to the bond makers heal her spirits,
She was always able to stand without him,
Though he thought it was cool and okay to no longer try,
It was him that appeared the fool,
Showing his reflection upon her,
It was just a mirage,
But the dark spot keeps growing in the pain,
The pain of her feeling a fool of believing him,
Her healing will start soon,
But it is only after she realizes the lesson,
Lesson that she was always stronger with her foundation,
He was just a wall of sand covered shells weakened with splash of life...

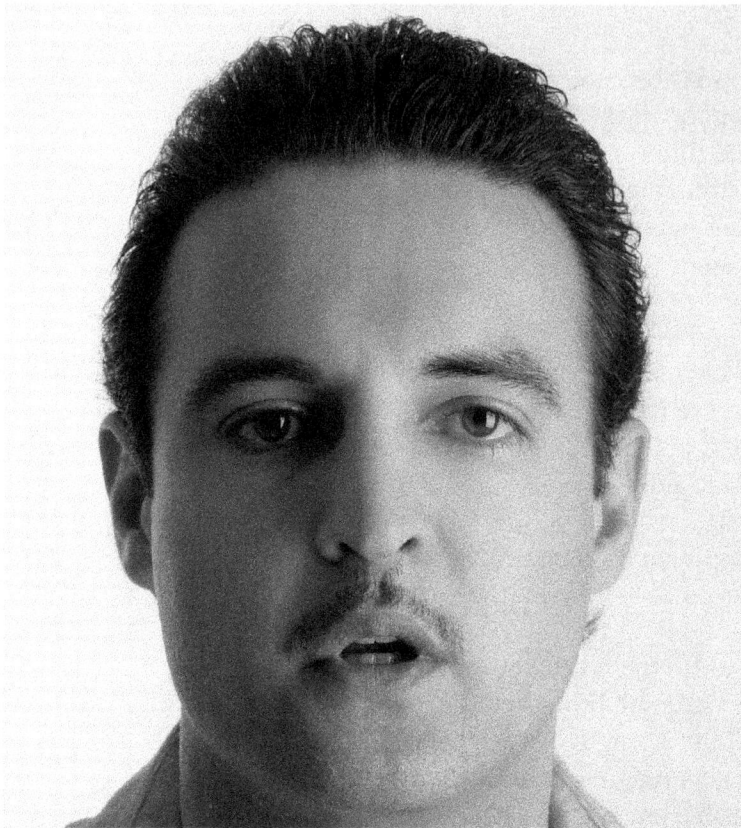

Amir Ali Samie Siassi

I'm an evolutionary child born during Iran's revolution. I was born September 24th 1979 in the U.S.A. Los Angeles, California is where I was raised. I came back to Iran when I was 11 years old and saw the after-effects of the Iran-Iraq war.

In my family there are Prime Ministers, Prime Ministers of Education, Mayors, etc. Also there are dervishes. I had the chance to be in the presence of dervishes. With the help of dervish Heydar Fulady, who was my grandfather's student, I learned to read and understand the poetry of Persia's finest poets. Rumi, Hafez, Sa'adi, Ferdowsi, Khayyam just to name a few.

IllumiNation

Luminaries in the world

Truthfully carry faith's torch

In the time of light, shine with a right-mind

Stars, start by blazing trails of bright insight

Sparks in flight, unite 2 ignite, one-pointedly aspire

And incite, enlighten "I's" out of sight to see the infinite

The **wise** actualize, realize and rise to recognize the eternal life

Any and Everything from the source or force of energy, Most High

Is entirely Above and completely Beyond measure

Solely the holy is to only be loved and wholly treasured

Forever is much more than any worldly fortune or pleasure

On Earth, of course, our work is to evolve as Blissful Beings of Consciousness, right

Career, Prosperity, Enjoyment & Liberation are the Goals of Life

The search begins by Believing, Conceiving, Achieving & then our works worth Receiving

The purpose creates greater reason to find deeper meaning

In the separateness & togetherness of Knower, Knowing & Known states of Being

Or Beloved, Love & Lover; ultimately in Unity seeing Multiplicity, in Multiplicity seeing Unity

Raj Aaryan

Name : Raj Aaryan :- Umang (Enthusiasm)

Age : 26, Living : New Delhi India

Qualification : Bachelor of Arts (Psychology honors)

Languages known : Hindi, English, Urdu, Punjabi

Work A Honorary administrator of "Fans of my poetry" a US based poetry group.

Working as senior consultant in a MNC based at New Delhi India

Awarded top performer of the year (2011) throughout country for best working skills.

The Mankind

Heat of Hate gives you nothing,
Flame of Love gives you something,

Beat the heat it's narrow & Filth,
Hold the flame
it's Broad & beautiful instinct,

Break out the dark of Jungle,
Stay cool polite & humble,

Only positiveness,
Hark back from tumble,

Golden tomorrow is not so far,
In-fact it's miles away from war,

Hit & hurt is easy,
Indeed it's tease,

So put your hands raise in prayers,
Not try to do misdeed's dare,
Easy is hurt,
But easier is care,

Heat of Hate gives you nothing,
Flame of Love gives you something,
Undoubtedly mankind gives you everything !!

…………I am just following it ..

Elizabeth Castillo

Elizabeth E. Castillo is a professional writer/journalist/blogger/international published author and poet from the Philippines in Asia. She was featured in more than 30 international poetry anthologies and a Contributing Editor for Inner Child the Magazine.

She has published an international poetry book "Seasons of Emotions".

http://seasons-reflections-of-the-muse.blogspot.com/?zx=255b56ec03eabc7b

Peace Starts Within Me

Almost all people want to change the world
But no one wants to change himself,
Leo Tolstoy once said
Out of the bruises and scars of society,
The permanent marks of crime and fatality
We always ask ourselves what's going on with humanity,
But have we ever pondered on and uttered "peace should start within me"?
Living in a world of chaos
Is not what the Almighty wants His beloved children to be in,
But to live in pure harmony, not shedding blood and tears
Caring for each other, no prosecution of our own brothers,
Delude envy with genuine love and erase each other's fears
Peace starts within me, I need to purify my soul first,
Before healing the ill world around me.
Hear the cry of even the unborn children
Of generations to come in bewilderment,
Prepare a world enveloped with love and contentment
Be good examples through good deeds and sincere words,
Say no to wars that leave no winners but just ugly scars
Stop selfish motives and be our brother's keepers,
Wake up to a renewed world clothed in PEACE, LOVE and LIGHT!

Alan W. Jankowski

Alan W. Jankowski is the award winning author of well over one hundred short stories, plays and poems. His stories have been published online, and in various journals including Oysters & Chocolate, Muscadine Lines: A Southern Journal, eFiction Magazine, Zouch, The Rusty Nail, and a few others he can't remember at the moment. His poetry has more recently become popular, and his 9-11 Tribute poem was used extensively in ceremonies starting with the tenth anniversary of this tragic event.

When he is not writing, which is not often, his hobbies include music and camera collecting. He currently resides in New Jersey. He always appreciates feedback of any kind on his work, and can be reached by e-mail at: Exakta66@gmail.com

http://authorsdb.com/authors-directory/1824-alan-w-jankowski

I'll Never Understand

The one thing I will never understand,
Is man's inhumanity to his fellow man,
How people who call each other sister and brother,
Could be so hurtful to one and other,
How people can treat each other so mean,
Without understanding where they've been,
Who would lead each other into war,
Choosing to be the problem, not the cure,
Who have the power to guide another man's fate,
With hidden agendas mixed with hate,
Who think nothing of causing another man pain,
If there is a dollar somehow to gain,
Who would send another man off to die,
While widows and orphans are left to cry,
Though they may play the part of an impartial judge,
They'll soon condemn you for some long-held grudge,
Stepping into the night like some heartless thief,
Their only goal is to bring another man grief,
Manipulating others they seek to control,
For a bit of power, they'd sell their soul,
Yes, the one thing I'll never understand,
Is man's inhumanity to his fellow man.

Laura Crean

Author of the children's fantasy novel 'The Realm of the Purple Dragon' and 'The Rainbow Rune Series'. Also poet, artist, blogger and reader and writer of the Science-Fiction, Fantasy and the Paranormal and Spiritual genres.
http://lauracrean.wordpress.com/poetry/

Bare Hands

With bare hands I sweep away the cobwebs of my life,
They hide the truth and cover the space restricting the view.
With bare hands I dig up the bones of my mistakes,
The dirt becomes embedded beneath my finger nails,
Marring their perfect, painted form.
With bare feet I walk the path of my ancestors,
Learning from their memories that every cobble counts.
With bare feet I feel the dusty road and negotiate each obstacle
That looms up in my way,
 each one a lesson in humility.
With bare chest I expose the home of love,
And with an open heart I share each broken vessel.
I invite you with a bare hand to touch my heart
and make it whole once more.
With bare hands held out and open
I extend my hand in honest friendship,
And with bare hands we join with one another
In a chain of unity that circles the earth
Like a halo of heavenly hands,
Each one a link of love and lessons learned.

~Keith Alan Hamilton~

~Keith Alan Hamilton~ is an independent online publisher, editor, poet/writer & Smartphone photographer.

http://www.keithalanhamilton.com

Email: webmaster@keithalanhamilton.com

do you believe ~

do you believe ~
have faith in…..
the power
of
We the people
working together
as a whole
united
to become
one humanity
focused on improving
the wellbeing of everyone
I believe ~
have faith in…..
the way
which leads
to everlasting joy
prosperity
health and peace
that responsibility
rests on the shoulders
of humanity
and no one else…..
We the people
must find the way
to help each other
help ourselves
so in turn
when helped
we then help others
on
and on
round
and round
we go

like the merry-go-round
until the ills of the world
are figured out
become no more…..
do you believe ~
have faith in…..
We the people
proactively working
together as one
where our legacy
will become ~
the great healer
the great peacemaker
of the world
'cause
We the people
of today
shall become
the leaders
have the foresight
to make the time
to increase
our Nature ~ IQ
intelligently progressing
so then
through our
acts and deeds ~
creativity
and technological
innovation
implemented
with adaptive
and transitional
concepts and practices
~ the struggle and effort
put forth in these actions
will bring forth the means

for us to transform
like the butterfly....
help ourselves
our children
and their children
into the future
to survive ~
by our developing
freely accessible
and affordable
~ energy
~ information/education
~ transportation
~ housing
~ health care
for all....
do you believe ~
have faith in.....
We the people

Carl Carr

Poet, Writer and Artist Õή a quest for healing, meaning and wholeness. My poetry has been published in the South African literary journals New Coin, New Contrast and Botsotso and in two Anthologies; 'Over the Rainbow' by New African Poets and 'Walking the Tightrope' by African Queer Poets.

E-MAIL: carlcarr166@gmail.com

BLOG: http://othervoices.blog.co.uk

THIS IS THE MOMENT

This is the moment
when fear flies
in the face of reason
the moment the womb rejects the seed
and violence invades
our perjury and treason
Crooked politicians and rabid priests
invade our TV space
and our computer and cell phone screens
dividing and exposing us to infiltration
by enemies who attack
our reality and dreams
Our walls are not high enough
our rusted locks cannot be closed
cannot be opened
alarms signal disasters
and invasions
that cannot be opposed
This is the moment
our prayers are left unanswered
and invocations chanted
within these city walls
call forth retribution
and hot coals fall
This is the only moment
that we have to live within
to carve out a meaning
to reason with the unreasonable
to die the death of heroes
or of saints

Deji Oladoye

Born in Kaduna, in 1985, Deji Oladoye studied Print-Journalism (Department of Mass Communication) at the Nigerian Institute of Journalism. He is a freelance journalist with National Daily Newspaper, a contributor on CP-Africa Online, Ventures Africa Magazine and a blogger.

As a poet and creative writer, Deji is inspired by people, nature, the environment, political drama, including the issues that pertain to limitations and greatness in the society. He is a writer who has contributed to various internet publishing sites.

Syria, you shall live again

Syria Shall Live Again
Your voice call from distance
Syria, you shall live again
Even if the moaning east wind tarry
And the deserts uplifted their heads
Heavenly feet above the Mediterranean tears

Syria, you shall live again
Above the hectic red rain; surge over you
And empty into the hungry sepulchre
The red sea not a messiah to your thirst
Dearly seek water from a barren desert
Whereas, the congregated white oceans chorus you
Their eyes locked in your storm

The vaccines brought to you fell
In the vapour of the red rain. Often
In the rude mud children refused to play in
Springs from your sisters' passion
For wife and children taste your pain
And their tongue died of saltiness

From the red rain who can preserve destiny
And wake with Damascus in your bear hands
Laying cold in the black winter
Without hot spirit to burn their wounds
On Homs, the harmony of cries
Your universal hunger for dirge
There is no feast of sepulchre too little
The multitude of red rain that empty down
Is a line in an early morning elegy
But you should chorus it
Before night falls the same way
Upon the Mediterranean kindred spirits

Your children and women not to seek safety
Under the earth eternal wrapper
If you must die, they should live
Above death sighs
Beneath the Mediterranean heightened breaths
The world spite bowl in the depth

Cheap, sophisticated for high currency
Chases the massacre of your man-made dust
Hideous forbidden death name
Ask if you are a father

And indeed, if a child pleaded your love
To the less, paper work pile up
Splitting your love like broken chain
Lives like the fame of your sister's pyramid

The fame for death
You should not be buried without a coffin
Without a tombstone
The pilo in the sleep of the earth
Said deaths were not sleeping peacefully

But, there is a shelter for your grave
A large political umbrella with death colour
To abort the red rain
From poisoning the Mediterranean love
For the sisters of the east. The lusty nostril
Gasp. That inhale, your man-made dust
Is your device. Sapless and sickening

Abominable sleeps in your womb
But you shall live again
Even if the mild east wind tarry
And the deserts uplifted their heads
Heavenly feet above the Mediterranean tears
Syria, you shall live again

Kerry Gans

Kerry is a write-from-home mom who squeezes in writing around her rambunctious preschooler. She writes middle grade and YA novels and short stories. She loves to write and will not stop until Death makes her. And after that…she may haunt a computer and keep writing anyway.

Contact link: klgwriter@aol.com

Website link: www.kerrygans.com

The Towers Stood

One summery September morning
Death flew out of the clear blue sky.
In Manhattan, papers and people fell like rain.
In Washington, the Pentagon crumbled.
In a Pennsylvania field, a plane of heroes crashed.

And still the Towers stood.
Flaming like the torch of Lady Liberty
They stood in defiance of hatred.

The enemy envisioned immediate collapse,
A domino effect of death.
But still the Towers stood.

American strength saved 16,000 people that day,
Although 2,977 perished, sudden soldiers
In an unexpected war.

On that day of death, there was no North or South
No coasts East or West
No difference between old money and new immigrant
No African-American, Asian-American, Euopean-American, Native-
American

On that day we were simply American,
United in anger and pain.
On the day the towers fell,
America rose.

Geri Algeri

Geri Algeri resides in Broadview Heights, Ohio, with her husband of 33 years. She is a non-denominational reverend, retired RN, mother, grandmother, and writer. Her lifelong passion for expressing through poetry began as an elementary school ecology assignment that won magazine publication. "Poetry is how my spirit breathes."

Geri Algeri can be reached at: GAlgeri@sbcglobal.net

And We Still Don't Get It

All enter the world,
And exit the world,
Penniless and alone,
Yet we fight as though
Power and wealth are eternal

From the wealthy to the indigent,
We all live and die,
Lose our loved ones,
Our health,
Our worldly things

Warmongering wealth,
And abusive power,
Are but symptoms,
Of poverty of spirit;
Humanity's terminal winter

Self-designated leaders haunted,
In solitude and dreams,
That which is eternal withers,
Isolated by guards and gold;
The price for greed

Nations rise and fall in bloodshed,
Under the Moon and Sun,
That ebb and flow,
In their commands,
Of vast sky

Allowing the seasons,
Of winter rests,
And summer yields,
Without celestial war,
They nurture all of life

Nature teaches us peace,
Lessons as big as the sky,
Shining o'er the world daily,
And we still don't get it,
Why?

Jon M. Nelson

As a poet that writes poems about peace and humanity, it was kind of difficult for me to narrow my selection down to just one poem, but I think I went with one that really has a powerful message.

My contact information: jonmnelson75@yahoo.com

My website: http://jonmnelson.com/

Pay It Forward

When you have the chance, lend a hand.

Don't be afraid to try to take a stand.

Pay it forward, expect nothing back.

Compassion is something we all lack.

A word of kindness is sometimes in need,

So is the chance to commit a good deed.

Pay it forward, take nothing in return.

Compassion is something we all can learn.

If you see the need, follow your heart,

Helping others out will always be a start.

Pay it forward and pass on the charity,

Compassion is out there, we all will see.

Help someone out with a life changing event,

Let someone feel that you were heaven sent.

Pay it forward, all the kindness inside,

Compassion is out there, it hasn't died.

Show your neighbor what they're worth,

And the reason that you're on this earth.

Pay it forward without ever any regret.

Compassion is here, let us not forget.

Roseville Nidea

Roseville Nidea is a Content Article Writer and aspiring poet from Philippines. She has been published in different anthology in USA and in Canada. Her passion to poetry is unceasingly growing; she yearns, too, to continue her ethnographic research to help preserve cultural practices and traditions.

House Sparrows

The sun was about to set
The house sparrows were all over
The lean branches of the evergreen mango tree;
At the balcony near the wild garden
I sat, on the corner of the old wooden chair
In silence, I listened to their voices--so sweet
So soft, so melodious
Nothing was more blissful than to hear
Them, singing in unison
A family of small brown-grey birds was gathering
Was sharing the comfort of their small home;
Before the night would take the light
They would all be shaded by the twigs
By the snug of the leaves of the unselfish tree.

Enchanted by the euphonious twits, I stretched
Both my legs reached, pressedhardly the rough ground;
The loud whistle of the kettle suddenly
Called my attention to return to the place
Where I prepared, where I cooked the food
To pour the boiled water into the slim, sky-blue thermo jar
That was for the black-brew of my king after dinner
And I must do it at once for after few strikes
Of the hand of the grey old clock
Hanging on the painted wall of the family room
He and our prince would again be home
Sure would seek the comfort of my tender hands.

And so, I went back inside the house
Before the night took the day –

Larry Miller Jr.

Capable of executing varying jobs in the world of performing arts: I act, sing, write (poetry, plays, and lyrics), direct (music and plays), am an accomplished musician (bass guitar, and African hand percussions), as well as, theater technician (lighting, sound, set carpentry.

Actor: 1989 – Present
Writer, Poet, Lyricist: 1989 – Present
Musician: 1989 – Present

I teach and/or coach from my home or travel to clients to train in either : Voice for the Actor or Singer, Acting Lessons, Directing, Play Writing and Editing Theatre and Music Production, Bass Guitar Lessons, Music Theory Music Composition, Lyricist, & Musical Arrangement

to my young'ns

too hard trying to be
than to simply be
the you of cosmic design
unfetered by the world's
one-sided'ness
to see yourself beyond it's description
you be the realness of what makes you breathe
to hell with all that refuse to see past the surface

maybe it simply be time to carve your
definition of self
of the man'ness
of what makes your heart pump
and your blood surge beneath your flesh

yes the craving for more than even your own imaginings
maybe it be time to let go of yesterday
work the sweat out of today
while pressing your way through to that
vision of tomorrow supernaturally inspired
preparations made to go to that place higher than I
best laid plans and their backups
bloody knuckles from the struggle
and being too stubborn to give up
frustration will not be a deterrent
done put up with too much
to shutup
get their sooner than me
knowing when what is necessary and
delivering all to the proper individual
and leaving the others alone
set the world a'blaze
see, go, move farther than I ever had
my young'ns
go,.....

Bozena Helena Mazur-Nowak

Bozena Helena Mazur-Nowak comes from Opole (Poland) and lives in London. The poet has released three volumes of poetry in Polish. In July 2013 her fourth book and first of selected poems in English, was released under the auspices of the IPPA, based in London. She is glad that her poetry is appreciated and also understandable to readers without "Polish roots."

She was invited by American poets, Lewis Crystal to participate in anthology "FM Summer 2013", "FM FALLS 2013" and Frances Ayers to e-book "Tender Words And Vibrant Songs". She is also a translator of poems by fellow Polish poets.

And it was yesterday

Years go by and memories are lost in the fog

But still are just as painful

Yellowed photographs so often nestled into the heart

Remind us that they lived among us

Grandma had a long number on the forearm

She often said that it was her name

Given her by the baptism of war

I listened to her story as a dark horror

Closed my eyes and looked trough grandmother's eyes

Eyes of a frightened child

Into the world that has been taken from her without her consent

Into that world she got though and did not want to

At night I pray for peace

I pray that my children never knew about hunger

And to be able to enjoy every moment

And that they can build a future as they desire

Mbizo Chirasha

Mbizo Chirasha is an internationally acclaimed Performance poet, Writer, Creative / Literary Projects Specialist, an Advocate of Girl Child Voices and Literacy Development. He is the Founder and Projects Curator of a multiple Community, Literary, and Grassroots Projects including Girl Child Creativity Project, Girl Child Voices Fiesta, Urban Colleges Writers Prize, and Young Writers Caravan.

In Memory Of Motherhood By Mbizo Chirasha ~ *Zimbabwe*

Pain scribbled signatures in mothers buttocks
announcing the beginning of sunset
sun rays remained un vomited from the beauty of rainbows
war tied ropes of struggle round their necks
many rhymes of suffering sung and unheard
in congregations marching townships and mountains
in search of freedom seeds
seeds of their wombs yearned for freedom far to be harvested
motherhood a definition of honesty hearts

with breasts carrying scars ,laughter ,smiles, and hope
those dimples signatures of resilience
thighs with grafitti of bullet bruises
valleys of their backs smell blood of sons,
sons long buried in the barrel of violence
life stolen in its greenness
motherhood her hands trust red clay soil , even
during cloudless seasons
the womb that breathe rays of this dawn ,today
scribbling this memory on the walls of the rainbow
Shoulders of motherhood carried journeys and hope
how many times hope die ,rise and ripe
erase propaganda from her shoulders
delete the baggage of slogan from from breasts
abort the luggage of war from her womb
bring pastures that she reap fruits of freedom
motherhood how many times you cough sorrow
how many seasons you sneeze hunger
you have eaten enough poverty
and licked the rough hand of war long unforgotten
motherhood freedom is now.

43

He was one of the innocent ones...
Standing on the byside.
But, these dumb asses... they don't quit.
At the enemy's grave site
They'll sit and sit,
Waiting and wanting,
Wishing and daring... 'somebody'
To come on with it.
'Because another mother******'s got to be wasted
Behind this shit!'
At after burial barbques,
Processed and SCurl fools
In Asian store bought jewels...
Are leading sermons 'bout...
'How one should live or die..'.
Standing around smokin'
Blunt rolled tokin'
Talking 'bout...
"Somebody's" dead body....
Is gonna pay some dues.
Paying dues...
Paying dues...
Paying dues...
Well, you ain't gonna here the KKK "Sing da blues..."
Because... just another black brother is dead ya'll...
By Black assassination.
Stop the violence. Choose or Lose LIFE.

Ashok Bhargava

Ashok Bhargava is award winning multilingual poet who has published four books of poetry. His poetry has been published in various literary magazines and anthologies. He is the founder of Writers International Network Society Canada (WINS), created to discover, nourish, recognize and empower writers and artists to assist them to network with the community at large.

PEACE

Peace comes green
to pallid plains
blood red azalea hills
burnt ashen rivers
orphaned children
widowed brides and
grief stricken people.

Peace comes as a golden flame
to the lost souls
they shield it with their cupped hands.

Peace comes as colorful threads
to the despaired refugees
they weave its delicate threads
into their dreams.

Peace comes as nectar
to thirsty hearts
they taste its dewdrops
with their tongues
as it drips
softly.

Neelam Saxena Chandra

Neelam Saxena Chandra has authored eight books including three poetry books, one novel and four books for kids. Besides this she has ten books in pipeline. More than 500 of her various stories/poems have been published in various national and international anthologies/journals etc.

https://www.facebook.com/pages/Neelam-Saxena-Chandra-Author-Poet/233802820120710

http://neelamchandra.wix.com/neelamsaxenachandra

THE CANVAS OF UNIVERSE

On the canvas of the universe
The portrait of peace
Drawn and painted
By the artist called Him
With a lot of care, caution and concern,

The colours of
Hatred
Biases
Violence
Intimidation
Radicalism
Sabotage
Look like defacing
The peace of the portrait of sanguinity
Seem to demolish
The edifice of love depicted on it.

Harmony
Is the key theme of the canvas
And let us join hands
To preserve it.

Joyce Nwanokwai

My name is Joyce Nwanokwai, hailed from the southern part of Nigeria delta state, studying criminology and security studies in the National Open University of Nigeria. Age 23. Started writing at the age of seven. Imagination to me is my inspiration.

Let peace over flow

Let peace over flow
Just like the water falls
Let it find its way into our hearts
O peace!
Peace perfect peace I speak
Let the stony heart be melted
And the broken heart be mended
Teach us no more to fight
For we are brothers in Christ
Rather I pray thee oh man
To wipe the tears in our eyes
And forget us not in distress
Least we fall weak into temptation
Oh…for how long shall we continue to war
Shouldn't we live without the missiles?
O peace!
Peace perfect peace I speak
Let all who seek freedom be free
And let the wounded souls be healed
For the time is come when the world will be at ease
When there will be no more tears to share but peace
O…Embrace peace for I speak in peace
Curse us no more to suffer
And suffer us no more to death.

Fikile Mosala

Fikile Mosala born and bred in South Africa, in Bloemfontein his a spoken word lover born 85-12-09. An author of poetry collection which will be release next year, his other work has been publish online, he is born a Poet.

Healing World

Thy mouth speak
Proclaim mighty acts
For they tell righteous deeds
Smile without a weep,

Thy words heal nation
Power for next generation,
For beauty star afar
Which brought health
Healing power to the earth,

The healing power,
Thee' is divinity
Favor of serenity
And ability to see goods,
Healing the world
With faith to hear the truth,
Courage to seek GOD's wisdom
A truth wisdom not as youth,

Tis love is caring
Sharing inner fear
And the courage to heal the world,
By watering the earth
With honest answers,
Like kiss on the lips
For all mouth will speak peace
And all to praise his glory
The world will be healed,

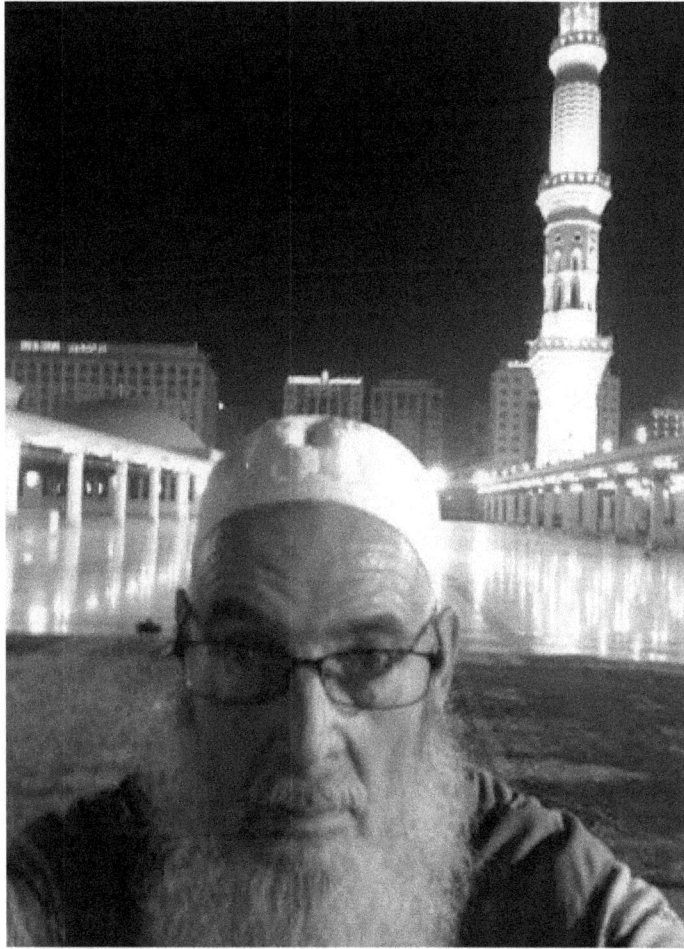

Shareef Abdur Rasheed

Born: BKLYN, NY (WW 2 Baby) / Raised: BKLYN, NY, Jersey City, NJ / Resided: BKLYN, NY, Jersey City, NJ, LI, NY, Tampa Bay Area, FL. / Education: BKLYN / COLLEGE, Suffolk County Com.College / Makkah, Saudi Arabia / Military Service: Viet Nam Era Vet / Reverted: Islam in Military 1969 / Active: Muslim Communities BKLYN & LI, NY, Civil Rights, / Participated, Sit ins "60's" Free Mandella, Bensonhearst / BKLYN(Yusef Hawkins Murder),Central Park case, Adam Abdul-Hakim case, Rasheed Family Case with Rev. Sharpton / Poetry: Since "60's" but inconsistant untill approx: one and a half years ago, Did some spoken word in College with Jazz group.Knew Sulaiman El Hadi and Jalal Mansor Nurraddin from original"Last Poets". We were in the Muslim Community in BKLYN, NY From 1969 to mid "70's" In several anthologies including "Gathering of words" "Anthology for Trayvon Martin" and "I want My Poetry To" published by Inner Child Press . . .

open...

up your mind
open up your heart
open up your soul
open up be kind
open up be whole
open up the lock
that imprisons
knowledge and wisdom
disguised by narrow minds
who try to hide the very
things by which we all
should abide!
open up the truth
hidden by lies
open up the cage and
let the song bird fly!
open up all things that
enrich!
undo the seal
rip the stitch
being real makes you
rich!
living without the contradict
all that's left after they flip
da script!
and leave like ratz jumping
off a sinking ship!
call dem out to take account
call their names aloud
open up your mouth and
shout
till dem come out from where
they hide!
to establish truth and crush the
lies!

food 4 thought!

Rosemarie Wilson

Rosemarie Wilson a.k.a. One Single Rose is an award winning poet, spoken word artist, singer, actress and playwright. She has self-published three poetry collections, performs nationally and internationally and hosts open mic poetry in the Spotlight at Manila Bay Café, 4731 Grand River in Detroit, Michigan every 1st and 3rd Friday. For more information on One Single Rose, please visit www.onesinglerose.com

She, Her, Me

I am the creator's daughter,
a spiritual being
blessed with a keen third eye functioning as her voice of reason.
I am a child of the atmosphere
bearing blood of her people that spilled throughout the land.
I am hope,
patiently waiting for comforting chords sung in harmony by every creature that has
breath,
tickled pink by peace as it fills a void left by chaos.
I am bilingual,
fluent in several dialects known to man,
well versed in the native tongue of our ancestors.
I am
she,
her,
me;
family in every sense of the word—
the sister who nags her siblings,
first, second and third cousin holding her kin down,
the aunt standing in for mom.
I am Fort Knox,
the confidant that knows but won't tell;
a friend who won't violate the code
or give up the key.
I am a girl playing hopscotch,
a woman doing Double Dutch;
a lady held in high regard.
I am the sweetheart
who became lover,
soon thereafter declared wife.
Mother of gifted stars,
companion to the world,
I am queen;
a bread winner,
head of the household
yet submissive when Mister takes charge.

I am tough—
the weight of earth lifted by these hands,
its burdens
buried beneath my smile
then carried across continents on these shoulders.
I am a frugal spend thrift wearing size 10 kicks,
stepping lively in the name of decency.
I am a heroine;
clumsily graceful,
yet beautifully built because I said so.
I am confidence deprived of arrogance
wading with humility.
I am love surrounded by hate,
joy
and pain
when the sun shines
or if it rains.
I am forgiveness with compassion for our souls
housing not one insidious bone
inside a frame that fails to turn green with envy.
I am she,
who loves her
because I know
I can only be
me.

J Katherine Carter – Russell

Writing has always been a big part of my life. By fourteen, I was writing stories of long lost lovers being reunited in a new life as they searched the Halls of Time. Music caught my fancy around this age; I began writing my song poems. I love writing period.
JkCarterRussell@Hotmail.com ~ http://www.youtube.com/user/artimuspartimus

World Peace

How can there be world peace
When you can't have good without evil
A safe neighborhood without police
Every individual must find the will
To always uphold the truest ideal
For the greater good
Remember the teachings of old
That should always be retold
The golden tool God sent to rule
Separates the gracious and the good
From those who never do what they should
How can there be world peace
Wars rage like vicious, hungry beasts
Sometimes you must fight and die to be free
To protect the children and the future you see
Maybe peace on Earth ain't meant to be
For the greater good
Remember the teachings of old
That should always be retold
The golden tool God sent to rule
Separates the gracious and the good
From those who never do what they should
Maybe we're here to learn
How to get on that bridge that's been burned
Battle the demons of sorrow and fear
Protect all that we love and hold so very dear
Rebuild that bridge that's been burned
For the greater good
Remember the teachings of old
That should always be retold
The golden tool God sent to rule
Separates the gracious and the good
From those who never do what they should
The golden tool separates the gracious and the good
From those who never do what they should.

Ty Gray-EL.

The 'Minister of Poetry' is an internationally renowned poet, storyteller and the founder of Breath of My Ancestors Cultural Enrichment Ministries. He is also Chief Creative Officer of Gray-EL Edutainment Media Syndicate, LLC. www.breathofmyancestors.com

One Man

If one man would make up his mind

to everyone he meet's be kind

and fix his heart on that which is true

If one man would be so bold

as to embrace the gospel and hold

just think what the strength of a million men could do

If one man changed his thought

each time the tempter brought

some selfish scheme that would his neighbor undo

If he thought for just a minute

just where is the kindness in it

just think what a million thoughts like that could do

If David could slay that giant

though huge and extremely defiant

and Solomon had the wisdom to think things through

If Shadrach could walk through fire

and his entire village inspire

just think what a million Shadrach's could do

If Noah could build that ark

though some people thought it a lark

and Jesus could cure those deaf and blind men too

If Sampson's strength was that of ten

ordinary men

just think what a million Sampson's can do

If one man would take a second

when his needy neighbor beckoned

and followed literally Moses' tenth command

With spirits filled and nourished

our neighborhoods would flourish

how quickly peace would spread throughout the land

If one man made up his mind

to no matter what, be kind

No matter what others might put him through

The strength of that man's resolve

would all our problems solve

And just think what a million men like that can do

Siddartha Beth Pierce

Siddartha Beth Pierce is a Mother, Poet, Artist, Educator and Art Historian. She has published and exhibited widely both nationally and internationally. Her first full length book of poetry and art, I Do, was released in November 2013 by inner child press.

An Angel's Voice of Reason

A resurrection
for the love and protection
of those folks
who did not believe
in the slaughter.
Instead, they prayed
where his head was laid
to bring back his soul
to wander
and heal the wounds
of those in pain
for many moons
to come.
And she was kept
near his heart
during his many hours
upon this earth
whether anyone
knew or not
the magic Mary one
Mother and lover
of old and new
assisted the disciples.
One by one
they led those
that had gone astray
the lame and tame
hurt and maimed
and raised their souls
to heaven.
Then evils reign
came to blame
the wonder of their hands
on devil's work
crossed out his name
and paid for fame
in ever burning fire.
While those that saw
and knew the Call

followed diligently
and in the end
goodness prevailed
with the birth of Christianity.
Yet there exists
many beliefs
Eastern and Western alike
that acknowledge Christ
yet follow their own paths
of righteousness
in the name of the Father and the Mother.
Whichever source
brings you closer to yourselves
accept those amongst you
who may wander
and eventually they will see
the Light within us all.
An angel's plea
I often hear
when I am falling asleep-
'Sweet dreams my dear,
We will abide by the Laws of Nature
and protect you here
on land and sea
forever be
with our Love Divine and True.'
The psalms are one
among many of our lovers
yet Buddha lived
to teach his Truths
and the Incas danced
the Cherokees romanced the Land
and all are One together.
People nationwide
earthly bound
and Universally accepted
will hear our song
that they belong
no matter how they see us
We are here
to bless you dears

chase away your fears
and hope that you might
work together
for Peace on Earth
is how we should abide together.
Now one and all
hear our Call
living and dead alike
arise each morn
and work for Love
and Enlightenment
and help those less fortunate
along your Way
and in the end
the Master's Plan
will be revealed
to one and all
that follow the steps
of kindness.
Threefold back you will
feel our assistance
as Karma works its magic
to bless you all
that heed our need
for forgiveness and assistance
in this earthly realm
where so many have gone astray
Stand strong
everyday
with conviction and vigor
whatever your name, your race, your creed
or gender
We love you so
each child of ours
from the richest to the poor
the meek and frail
the strong and bright
equally will prevail
each day and every night.

Charles Banks

Charles Banks took a poetry class that kicked off his writing. Though Mr. Banks attended Devry University for computer technician, he has been writing since 1970s going full time in 2008. Having a passion for the craft, he wanted something that would compliment his artwork as well. He is known by his peers as Charles Seabe Banks or Seabe. One can find Mr. Banks works throughout the internet and other publications. The humorous but serious poet is known reading others works to assist in his artistic growth. He currently resides in Houston, Tx.

BlOOd

were not for the blood
we would be invisible...
crimes of life reveal us... so..
divisible as we are...
Hate peels us back...
lay bare souls
wondering love when
where if exposed...
no acre of land
is not stained
useless flowers on
a fresh grave
and the carry goes... on
for eons...time doesn't
change that...it flows
to the seas ...rivers
no covers remain..
that are not befouled
innocence is a shell
we are born from blood
skins soaked in it
we taste it...
pain yell of it..
on the first day breath..
breathe a bit ...
and scream...
wondering when where if
this love were fore told...
poetic epilogue . . .
he sits views the world
outlook panes shade him
fat pinkish blueish dropps
slowly blood reDD
the people like cRaBs
gather/ climb up a bucket
their actions paints them
knifes swing
blood the rain...
blood the rain
they're own making..

Racquel Robertson

I am a 20 year old poet, I have been writing since age 12, and started performing at age 18 for my church. I currently attend The University of the West Indies, Mona, Jamaica. In addition to poetry I also dance - I consider these talents, my ministry for God's Kingdom.

A Letter From The Abused

You want to know what hurts worse?
You want to know what kills me inside?
You want to know why I so desperately want to commit suicide?

Its not just because you verbally accuse me for you inability to stand straight
After a night at the bar.
Its not just because you remind me constantly of how
Worthless,
Uncaring,
Unworthy,
Ugly,
Stupid or
Unwanted I am.
It's not just because you invade my body with your whip,
Every night causing me to bleed and swell, like a Christmas pig,
It's not just because the bruises won't heal, the blood won't stop running,
The black and blue eyes will no longer open.
No! It's not just because your friends visit me every night, having their way with me,
Showing off their might... even though I just lay there without putting up a fight.

I don't only hurt because your unrestful angry spirit,
Your restless abusing hands, your unkind daggers of words attack me everyday
Leaving my body, my face, my spirit unidentifiable!
NO!
NO!
NO! It's not just because he left us to fend for ourselves and you blame me for your mistakes of running him away!

..... It's not because you lock me away for days only visiting to fulfill your needs to beat...
What hurts the most.... is that you never.....
Never....
Never....
.....You never said you loved me....

Tribhawan Kaul

Born in J&K/India on 01-01-1946, I am a freelance published poet having authored "Children of Lost Gods'/2013 and getting published in various anthologies, books and websites. My poems are basically a journey to the kingdom of poetry through the inspiring feelings absorbed and observed of the happenings within my country, around me and in the world giving wings to my creative imagination.

Tribhawan Kaul
Freelance writer-poet
e-mail: kaultribhawan@yahoo.co.in
Blog: www.kaultribhawan.blogspot.in

Soul searching by peace

Standing before the mirror gazing self
twin one croons,
"history of wars, fights, skirmishes
have already taken toll of you
terrorism of every dimension
now becoming sin number eight
what is to expect now from you ?"
It questions simple and straight.

"Sometimes you are scarred
Sometimes you are battered
Sometimes you are crossed
Sometimes you are martyred.

So
Are you dead ?
Nay, I dread
you are not yet,"
whispers my mirrored friend.

"eighth sin has no place
war has no grace
let more sunshine be there
for everyone and everywhere
undoing mean human mentality
let darkness not prevail
blinding us till eternity."

"Rise, rise, rise once again
show your prowess
hold tightly drooping reins
peace, humility and harmony breeds
great civilizations
don't dump into dustbins
God's own beautiful creations."

"Alias love, compassion and brotherhood
you can't be dead
wake up and change the mindset
for the sake of entire humanity
make violence to shed violence
apartheid to shed bias
states to terminate conflicting ways
with false vanity
and embrace you
with heart and soul
global peace be only your goal."

Could withstand no more
allowed it to merge in mine
my conscience ready to take on
all the violent ways head on
for peace and harmony.

Hilda Wales

Hilda Wales, Albuquerque, NM, retired from the United World College in Montezuma, NM, where she served as counselor and coordinated a curriculum on Constructive Engagement of Conflict for international students. She lived ten years in Latin America, among other sojourns, Her poetry is published in a variety of venue.

COLLECTIVE PARDON

Words are too fragile
will not—cannot—purge the pain
of last year's words,
words we carved on stones
now fossilized and silent
in the mountains of your memory
where even careful mining
cannot extract the poison.
To whom do we say, "We are sorry"
and who do we forgive?
We cringed behind our bolted doors
as certain that you stole our safety
as you are sure we seized,
we crushed, your freedom.
Our own memory mountain
still reeks in every fissure.
Every chasm smells of fear
stinks of hate.
Whenever we wander
through these isolated hills,
we hasten home to bunker,
foxhole, condo, migrant camp,
afraid of what can happen next.
So we speak the words of sorry.
Do with them as you will.

Ceri Naz

Caroline Nazareno, Ceri Naz to her friends and numerous followers, is a poet, journalist, public speaker, linguist and educator. Noticed for having raised the bar of her art, she was invited as a featured poet at Vancouver Word On The Street and World Poetry Canada and International. She was likewise an active participant in Poetry Reading at World Poetry Night Out New Westminster, British Columbia, Canada. She was awarded Empowered Poet 2013 by World Poetry Canada and International during the International Peace Festival on May 2013.

http://thecherrymuse.blogspot.com/2013/09/beautiful-words-by-beautiful-soul-ceri.html

http://worldpoetry.ca/?p=1963

http://www.pinoyparazzi.com/filipina-poet-gains-intl-recognition/

where peace can be

million years of ifs and buts
eloquently circulating in many tongues
crossroads of meanings read aloud
but found meaningless.
unheard. unseen. unrealized.
should it just be a theme to write about?
a blockbuster movie to queue up
should i play the role
of a gladiator
a hero
a warrior
a prize fighter
a soldier?
and broadcast a nation address
"now is the total absence"
of combats, of chaos, and bloodshed
does it mean safe and sound?
when my brothers are homeless and dead?
always been a missing piece
it's nowhere.
the ceasefire
is in the heart
of human race.

Nbada Sibanda

Ndaba Sibanda is a Zimbabwean-born writer. He hails from Bulawayo, Zimbabwe`s second largest city. He is one of the most prolific poets to emerge from that Southern African country.

A former National Arts Merit Awards (NAMA) nominee, Ndaba's poems, essays and short stories have been published in Africa and the US. His latest anthology, *The Dead Must Be Sobbing* was published in March 2013. Ndaba`s debut novel, Timebomb has been accepted for publication in the UK.

He lives in Saudi Arabia.

http://www.africabookclub.com/?s=Ndaba+Sibanda

Patience is a must

I will be calling each of you who have

Come to this earth to remind you that

People aren`t electrons and, so don`t

Expect them to behave in the same manner

Under similar conditions, they won`t!

Don`t be shocked if you show them love

And they flash at you unconcealed hate

Be glad that at least they `re true to you!

Some were taught by parents to smile

Whenever possible, but they frown

Even if it isn`t called for and strenuous!

I know you aren`t virtuous, either

But try to be patient and people-wise!

Again, I do respectfully and thankfully

Ask for your patience in this regard!

Deb Smart

Deborah Wilson Smart is a Publishing Consultant with One Smart Lady Productions and lives in Southern New Jersey. She is the author of "Joy Comes Through the Mourning" published by Gladstone Publishing Services. Deborah works with new and emerging authors to help them fulfill their dreams to become published authors.

Through Apathy Comes A Path to You

Through Pain Comes Anger
Through Destruction comes Pride
Through Selfishness comes Arrogance
Through Self-Awareness comes Truth
Through the Word of God comes Healing
Through Redemption and Reconciliation come You
Anger withholds the truth.
Pride resists the truth.
Arrogance blocks compassion and mercy, yet
Truth takes away weapons of hate and self-destruction, when
Healing removes the wedge between the loved and unloved; then
You find yourself on a new path.
This path leads to complete Healing and Love.
This path opens your heart to others pain.
This path allows you to be whole
Whole like you were at birth.
No prejudice, no hate.
Whole like you were before the abuse.
Mental, physical, spiritual and emotional abuse.
Whole to be the individual God meant for you to be.
Lacking nothing, desiring everything; freely expressing you.
This path paves the way for a new beginning.
Like the rivers Tiger and Euphrates when the earth was born.
Your rebirth from apathetic soul to healing soul is the secret, to
World Healing and World Peace.

Wayne Lee

Wayne Lee (wayneleepoet.com) lives in Santa Fe, New Mexico. His poems have appeared in *Tupelo Press, The New Guard, Sliver of Stone, Slipstream,* and other publications. Lee has been nominated for a Pushcart Prize, and his third collection, *The Underside of Light* was published by Aldrich Press in October 2013.

Order my new poetry book, The Underside of Light

visit my website at http://www.wayneleepoet.com/

Sign of the Cross

Priest: Though a missile may be any thrown or launched object, it colloquially almost always refers to a self-propelled guided weapon system
The people rise and reply:
The word missile comes from the Latin verb mittere, meaning "to send"
Then, if appropriate, the Deacon, or the Priest, adds:
Warheads are most commonly of the high explosive type, often employing shaped charges to exploit the accuracy of a guided weapon to destroy hardened targets
All pray in silence with the priest for a while
At the words that follow, up to and including and became a man, all bow
To indicate the end of the reading, the reader acclaims:
Warheadless missiles are often used for testing and training purposes
The Priest, standing at the side of the altar, washes his hands, saying quietly:
Shorter-range developments have become widely used as highly accurate attack systems
After this, the Priest, bowing profoundly, says in a low voice:
Most famous of these are the V-1 flying bomb and V-2, both of which used a simple mechanical autopilot to keep the missile flying along a pre-chosen route
In Masses for the Dead, the following may be added:
This job can also be performed somewhat crudely by a human operator who can see the target and the missile
And, striking their breast, they say:
The latest heat-seeking designs can lock onto a target from various angles, not just from
Then follows the Communion Rite
The Priest says to the communicants:
These systems have continued to advance, and modern air warfare consists almost entirely of missile firing
At the end the people acclaim:
The guidance is for relatively small deviations from that

Kathamann

I am a returned Peace Corps Volunteer/Afghanistan and a retired registered nurse. I paint, draw and make 3D objects. I've been writing poetry for 10 years, participate in occasional public readings, and have been published in many regional anthologies.

Socorro Strewn with Pumpkins

Our favorite downtown cactus
full of flirting spiders.
Tall columns of dust demons
spin into homes.
The purple soul of the goddess
bequeaths treasures of rain.

Every picnic will be disrupted.
Waterfalls will form at irregular
intervals.
Voices alive with candy bars
will sing with the angels.
Golden copper apricots will
become the new currency.

Dances will be held in the muddy
ballpark. Silent neighbors will
embrace for the first time in 34
years. Peace will descend like
music.

Gifts will be exchanged. Grace
will erupt like a sneeze. Insightful
speech will echo up ad down the
camino. Pockets full of hearts
will weep from happiness.
The light of the day will interrupt
in a new clarity.

Vanessa Barthel

Inspirational Speaker, Poet, Author Vanessa Barthel did not discover her passion for writing until her mid forties. Known to many as Poetess Vee Styles, her love to inspire never wavers. With compassion and her own life experiences, the Author writes to enlighten even the most hollow Soul. Given the words and vision for A Soul Recharged, which is her up incoming book, The Author never wavers on inspiring others. The Author currently resides in Atlanta, Georgia where she is working her first novel *A Love Story*

Color of Love

Love
the most misused
word in the
world.

Some get it
confused with lust.
Some even believe
it not real
unless it hurts.

People spend A
lifetime searching
for it, yet too blind
to see it.

This four letter word makes
some uncomfortable
solely because their minds
do not understand how
two Souls of different race
or same sex could truly
be Mates.

The truth of the matter is,
Love is not black or white,
straight or gay, painful,
unsure, money nor manipulation.

Instead, genuine real love is a combination
of many delightful colors!

Love is divine. Love is commitment. Love is patience.
Love is peace. Love is joy. Love is understanding.
Love should be you and I.

Rosaliene Bacchus

Rosaliene Bacchus is a Guyana-born writer living in Los Angeles, California, who hopes the day is coming soon when we can put aside our differences to work together as one to save ourselves from our self-destructive way of life.

Contact: admin@rosalienebacchus.com
Writer's Website: http://rosalienebacchus.com/writer/TheJourney.html

Yes, We Can

The time has come
to put aside our differences,
to work together as nations.
Yes, we can.

The time has come
to live within our means,
to say no to false promises of gain.
Yes, we can.

The time has come
to live responsibly as citizens,
to care for our planet and its resources.
Yes, we can.

The time has come
to be our brother's keeper,
to give hope when all seems lost.
Yes, we can.

The time has come
to be the change that we need,
to forge a better world for generations to come.
Yes, we can.

Regina Ann

Regina Ann is the founder of Integrative Wholistic Solutions, a holistic health and wellness center, and Bentz Talent Agency, Oklahoma's exclusive all digital talent agency bringing talent and production together. Along with her Twin Flame Soul Mate, Rich Bentz, she co-hosts the Empowering Transformation Radio Show each week on Inner Child Radio. She is also the Editor of the Health & Wellness section of Inner Child Magazine and mother of three sons. Learn more about Regina at :
http://integrativewholisticsolutions.com/

It Begins With Me

When World Peace is what I seek

I must accept…it begins with me

when I hold that space of peace

fully within each heart beat

resonate peace energy

emit peace frequency

peace travels forth

as a ripple on a pond

peace washes over my family

my neighbors, my community

and as each one vibrates

at that peace rate

the peace they emanate

washes over their family

their neighbors, their community

until all the world is awash

in the peace frequency

and so you see

world peace…it begins with me

Fidel M. Love

Fidel M. Love is a poet/author born on the southside of Chicago. He started writing poetry and fiction at a young age, and self published his first book of poetry, "Cry Through The Pen" in 2012. https://www.facebook.com/fidel.m.love

World Apart

I live in a world apart
And still feel the pain
of people wishing for change
who live a world apart
Cause' we're all—a part
of this world
I never want to see another hurt
We're all children of Mother Earth
We all answer to Father Time
My brothers –
No one can live forever
so why bother trying
All we have is us
All we have is now
I'm tired of wondering why
So all I'm asking is how…
Long will we allow
the poison to seep into our veins
And let the brainwashing images
enter deep into our brains
That tell us we are different
And none of us are the same
So when the world's going insane
We just shake our heads and ask,
When's the world going to change?
Cause' in our hearts
We feel that we aren't a part of it
But things will never begin to change
If we aren't the start of it
We may never live forever
but what we leave behind
should be a sign
of the beauty of our time
By what we did together

Steven Thompson

My name is Steven Thompson. I am a freelance writer that words hard everyday to help others in need and mostly to obtain my dream of world peace. I am in the photo listed in the front row, the man wearing black. There we are accepting our Character awards.

Under The Wings Of Life

Dark clenches a man's soul setting him upon the hell fire's bowl.
The weak will struggle, the strong will succeed.
Never regret a person in there time of need.
A battle comes raging forth each taking the disasters differently.
Through our pain we rise to gain our knowledge, for we do not know pain is the beginning of peace.
The pain is gift from our father above, our real test is world peace knowing suffering exists.
Do not hesitate dear young friend, for peace will find you in the end.
To obtain is to know great amounts of pain, for you can help someone's way.
Peace is simple, yet somehow complex where all the turns neglect our aspects.
In order to rise we must stand as bothers like those of locked links upon the prison.
Hold up your faith upon your beliefs, for all of us done what we thought is right.
Our behaviors towards peace reflect our past happenings, for we do not ask them what they endure, instead we simply judge and go about our ways, hoping they can heal themselves another day.
The hate rises even further from our foolish decisions, for we do not help others to ease the pain, the hate inside them takes over their plan.
Through raging fault the man demands a new world order to cease that plan.
He hurts and may kill the others around, for he does not see his former plan.
He does what has been done to him to avenge his love, for his city, family and the ones who died.
He gives war a hell of a ride, until we are all done. That is when peace arrives.
The war is not a true way to peace, however the pain inflicted upon one is what makes it unique.

Vincent Van Ross

I am a journalist, writer, editor and photographer. I am based at New Delhi in India. I write in English and Hindi. I write news and feature stories; short stories, poems and humour. I write on a variety of themes including national and international politics, defence, environment, travel, spirituality etc.

HASTY CONCLUSIONS

Someone
Sent me a message
And asked me
To take a look at it!

I tore open
The envelope,
Emptied the content,
Spread it on my table
And, yelled:
That
Was a blank paper
You sent!

If only
I had turned
The page over,
I would have seen
What he told me—
That the message
Was on the other side!

Life
Is full of
Such hasty conclusions!

Larry F. Nigh

Larry F Nigh has been writing for about two years. Previous to that he worked in numerous jobs. Now he is becoming an author. He is an actor on the stage. He holds a BA in English, and an MA in Geography.

Birds Can Fly In The Rain

Birds can fly in the rain,
The strong can live with pain.
Whatever may befall
One's heart can bear it all.
Loses come to the best,
Even saints have no rest.
Blessings will come again.
When one allows them in.
Joy returns in its time.
Without reason or rhyme.
Only wait for the day,
True peace will come your way.
Blessings will come to those
Whose soul is like a rose,
Blooming with true beauty,
As one did one's duty.
One can live with grieving
At the loss, the leaving
Of loved friends and others,
Siblings, fathers, mothers.
Lost to hearts forever.
No, they leave us never.
In our young one's faces
We can see the traces
Of the ones who left us,
May it always be thus.

Mary Carroll – Hackett

Mary Carroll-Hackett's book The Real Politics of Lipstick won Slipstream's 2010 poetry competition, and her chapbook Animal Soul was released in 2013 from Kattywompus Press. Her newest collection, If We Could Know Our Bones, is due out from A-Minor Press in January 2014. She is currently working on a memoir.

Contact Link: http://poetryattheporches.wordpress.com/

Website Link:

http://writingforpeace.org/about/writing-for-peace-advisory-panel/mary-carroll-hackett/

If We Could Know Our Bones

But if you do not know yourselves, then you live in poverty.~Gospel of Thomas

If we could know our bones the way we know our skin, perhaps we'd not dig graves, but build rooms, havens, shrines, for even our enemies, their bodies rescued from the ditch and battlefield, no longer pitched into holes, safe and out of sight, but standing, eloquent and equal in their lines: tines of rib, cradle of skull, clavicle like a little key, memories of movement in femur and fluted tibia, their jaws, hinged and singing, angel light pouring through the basin of each pelvis. Free of water, fat and muscle, perhaps they'd claim us, tell us of sharing even what can't be known – Os innominatum – those nameless bones.

Lennart Lundh

Lennart Lundh was discharged from the military as a conscientious objector in 1970. His work as poet, historian, short-fiction writer, and photographer has appeared internationally since 1965.

lenlundh@aol.com

Later Evolutions

Were there men or women

still, they might discuss, dissent

Darwin's insight or some gods' intentions

as to modifying

miracles and mercies,

and after all the words would wonder

at the Monarchs on high honeysuckle

bowing in the breezes,

for the butterflies sing now

with such strong, sweet voices

in the silences we left.

Shirani Rajapakse

Shirani Rajapakse is a Sri Lankan poet and author. She won the Cha "Betrayal" Poetry Contest 2013. Her collection of short stories, Breaking News (Vijitha Yapa 2011) was shortlisted for the Gratiaen Award. Shirani's work appears in, Cyclamens & Swords, Channels, Linnet's Wings, Spark, Berfrois, Counterpunch, Earthen Lamp Journal, Asian Cha, Dove Tales, Buddhist Poetry Review, About Place Journal, Skylight 47, The Smoking Poet, New Verse News, The Occupy Poetry Project and anthologies Short & Sweet – an anthology of Sri Lankan Hint Fiction (forthcoming 2014), Music Anthology (forthcoming), Poems for Freedom, Voices Israel Poetry Anthology 2012, Song of Sahel, Occupy Wall Street Poetry Anthology, World Healing World Peace 2012 and Every Child Is Entitled to Innocence. She blogs rather infrequently at :

http://shiranirajapakse.wordpress.com.

Peace

We planted a tree;
a little mango tree, at the
side of the lawn in the front
garden. A tiny shoot stuck its head
out of the flower pot that was its home
until that day. Little yellow green
leaves peered out at the world, curious
like kindergarten students, staring in
wonder and amazement
at everything around, laughing
at the sun, playing with the soft warm
winds bending, caressing as they
moved across the land. The little
tree grew up tall
and strong. The leaves changed
colour and shape, turning dark green
and thick. The tree rose up high to claim
the sky, like your hands reaching
out to grasp mine living here in a different
country; it spread its roots deep to claim
the earth, to be one
with all beings, big and small
seen and unseen, dark and light. White
flower buds peeped out eager to bear
fruit in abundance to feed us. The

branches spread across
the garden, leaves fluttered
in the tropical breeze blowing
across the land murmuring messages
of peace to the winds that took it
far, far away to the mountains,
the valleys between and the regions
we don't know. Over the gate
and past the road
to the next village it went. The
branches clawed the sky rising up
high, high, high, as if to caress
the stars. Powder puff clouds beckoned
then stood back in awe. Our tree
had grown so. It touched the world
and all around just like
we will if you give us a chance.

Kolade Olanrewaju Freedom

Kolade is a Nigerian poet and essayist who aims at healing the world with words. He has his poems published in diverse international anthologies and magazines.

Links:
https://www.facebook.com/kolade.olanrewaju
https://www.larryfreedom.blogspot.com

The Light In words

An 'iroko' is not cut with a single cut
A mountain is not climbed with a single climb
A dying world can be revived
Not with a word
But with words that are triggers;
Catalysts of positive deeds

I have chewed kola-nuts from dawn to dusk
Silently praying that peace be restored
Yet my eyes will not sight peace
In her beautiful regalia
Yet my ears will not hear peace sound roaringly
Like the voice of many waters

Why should peace suffer the world
Like an 'abiku' in the hand of a widow?
Nay! I say nay!
Our deeds as humans are inhuman
And with our own hands
We stab peace right in her heart
By denying love in our heart

When words become swords
Blood is not shed but light is shed
The unknown made known
The right way to tread
Is lighted for all to see
Stolen peace kept in darkness
Is restored by the light in words

'Abiku' is a yoruba word which means predestined to death.

Richa Dixit

Country :- India

Email:- richa23dixit@gmail.com

Reasons to smile

Sitting on the sands ,

In that full moon open black sky,

Adoring the sea waves that touch my feet and go by,

Though silence spread,

Still feel my heart humming for self ,

All was enough to give a reason to smile,,,,,,,,,,

No glitters of gold,

No silver sparks,

Still my eyes behold shines,

Counting the sea tides,

Though not fetching me a penny,

Still is enough to give a reason to smile,,,,,,,,,,,

Building small sand houses,

With some vague iffy architectures ,

Though not seems as mansion,

Though not seems as banglaw ,

Still is enough to give a reason to smile,

Those dolphins of the sea,

Though i don't know them,

Nor do they know me,

Still it seems,

They jump,

They dive on & on,

As in a purpose to entertain me,

They making sounds ,

Don't know what they mean ,

Though this not serving me as music,

Still is enough to give a reason to smile,,,,,,

Turning back from the sea and the sands,

Felt at heart deep inside,

As if this an hour was the best of life

Though was alone,

Mates were just these pebbles,

Throwing them in the sea,

'as if some wish coins,

Didn't made me any riches for sure,

Still enough to give reasons to smile,,,,,,,,,,,,,,,,,,,,,,,,,,,,,,,

epilogue

a few words from ... *hülya n. yilmaz*
Ph.D., Liberal Arts

The 30th anniversary of the founding of the United Nations was marked, among other tributes across the globe, by the Cantata *An die Nachgeborenen, op. 42* Gottfried von Einem had composed to honor the international organization's mission. On the 24th of October 1975, New York hosted the premiere of this opus for which the source was the poem, "An die Nachgeborenen" ("To Those Who Follow Our Wake") by Bertolt Brecht. This three-part poetic construct evidences the author's allusions to the terror-filled Thirty-Years War and World War I. The intensification of the battle forces across Europe in 1939 – the time when the Brechtian verses are known to have surfaced, the looming sufferings of World War II seem transparent to the poet. He thus resorts in this timeless piece to the collected wisdom of humanity and alerts the next generations of readers against silence in face of adversity:

> Truly, I live in dark times!
> An artless word is foolish. A smooth forehead
> Points to insensitivity. He who laughs
> Has not yet received
> The terrible news.
>
> What times are these, in which
> A conversation about trees is almost a crime
> For in doing so we maintain our silence about so much wrongdoing!
> And he who walks quietly across the street,
> Passes out of the reach of his friends
> Who are in danger?

The poem's second part uncovers Brecht's tragic confession, as "[t]he time given to [him] on earth" has passed with him failing to reach the goal for humanity: the spread of knowledge against the infectious mentality behind the war. His verses in the last part, then, assume the tone of a will. The author pleads yet once again with the arriving generations for their retreat from the conflicts of the world, in remembrance of the senseless violence and terror of life the war inflicts on humanity:

You, who shall resurface following the flood
In which we have perished,
Contemplate –
When you speak of our weaknesses,
Also the dark time
That you have escaped.

For we went forth, changing our country more frequently than our shoes
Through the class warfare, despairing
That there was only injustice and no outrage.

And yet we knew:
Even the hatred of squalor
Distorts one's features.
Even anger against injustice
Makes the voice grow hoarse. We
Who wished to lay the foundation for gentleness
Could not ourselves be gentle.

But you, when at last the time comes
That man can aid his fellow man,
Should think upon us
With leniency.

For Brecht, one of the most critically acclaimed world poets of German birth, to offer an autopsy of systematic programs of silencing and mass destructions seems ironic. For, the English word 'war' originates from 'Werran' in the Old High German language ('Werre' in Old English). As for its etymological meaning, the word's outreach capacity disappoints: to confuse or to cause confusion. In its political context, however, it reveals a state of armed conflict; or, as Carl von Clausewitz, the Prussian military analyst defines it, "continuation of politics carried on by other means."

Conflicts carried on by arms – whether in a state of confusion – have been an integral element of world history. Before what became to be the first recorded war between Sumer and Elam in 2700 BCE, tribes had been fighting against one another for thousand of years. The historian, Simon Anglim notes:

A tribe is a society tracing its origin back to a single ancestor, who may be a real person, a mythical hero, or even a god: they usually view outsiders as dangerous and conflict against them as normal. The possession of permanent territories to defend or conquer brought the need for large-scale battle in which the losing army would be destroyed, the better to secure the disputed territory. The coming of 'civilization' therefore brought the need for organized bodies of shock troops.

Inherent in the dichotomic 'self' and 'other' relation, therefore prompting fear of a different culture the tribe mentality has been known to often result in war, when a desire to expand was present. With the advancing of technology, war – as can be observed further, spread confusion throughout the ages, indeed reflecting the origins of the word.

While war continues to be a frequent extension of political disputes in the 21st century, as not only stimulated but also justified by the ancient tribe mentality, history of literature throughout time accentuates teachings to the contrary. As early as in the era of the Latin poet Albius Tibullus (ca. 55 BC – 19 BC), humanity's capacity for self-destruction has been questioned and the passionate call for peace has been recorded:

War is a Crime
Whoe'er first forged the terror-striking sword,
His own fierce heart had tempered like its blade.
What slaughter followed! Ah! what conflict wild!
What swifter journeys unto darksome death!

Come blessed Peace!
Come, holding forth thy blade of ripened corn!
Fill thy large lap with mellow fruits and fair!

Elegies, Book I, Number XI

Who was he, who first forged the fearful sword?
How iron-willed and truly made of iron he was!
Then slaughter was created, war was born to men.
Then a quicker road was opened to dread death.

What madness to summon up dark Death by war!
It menaces us, and comes secretly on silent feet.

Then come, kindly Peace, hold the wheat-ear in your hand,
and let your radiant breast pour out fruits before us.

Elegies, Book I, Number X

117

Literary history offers untiring pleas to humanity against the adoption of the tribe mentality and implores world's attention to the anguish of the people during and after the wars preceding our lifespan. Advanced technology with its growingly more destructive products continues to rule over the 21ˢᵗ century. Opposing nations or combating groups within the same national structures are resolved to leave ensuing centuries their violence-conditioned inheritance. Voicing the obvious anew seems to be of vital importance at our times when there still is an audience. "[S]o why do I tell you/anything?" reads the first line in the last stanza of the Adrienne Rich (1929-2012) poem, "What Kind of Times Are These." The poet further composes: "Because you still listen, because in times like these/to have you listen at all, it's necessary/to talk about trees." The intent behind Rich's lyrical work is, as to be expected, not to "talk about trees" but rather, through an imagined common language, to arrive at human love. In the commitment to get to human love – the pivotal subject of any personal or social order, lies the inspirational seed of the *World Healing World Peace 2014, a Poetry Anthology*. The heart and mind behind it can best be told – yet once again – within the framework of literature and its role that is as vital as life itself.

The name of a French dramatist, novelist and essayist is marked as the first writer in Europe to raise his voice against the war: Romain Rolland (1866-1944), the recipient of the Nobel Prize for Literature in 1915. Maxim Gorky (1868-1936), who founded the Socialist Realism literary method, had identified his contemporary within the context of humanism against "the horrors of the slaughter of 1914-1918":

> People say that Romain Rolland is a Don Quixote. To my mind that's the best thing that one can say about anybody. In the great game played by the forces of history with no compassion for us people, a man who craves fairness is also a force, and as such he is capable of opposing the spontaneity of this game. […] In *L'âme enchantée* his heart tells him that soon another, kinder truth the world has long needed will be born. He feels that a new woman will be born to replace the one that is now helping to destroy this world – a woman who understands that she must stimulate culture and therefore she wants to enter the world proudly as its lawful mistress, the mother of men created by her and answerable to her for their acts.

With his conception of the present poetry volumes, Williams S. Peters Sr. justly claims a place in the company of his literary forerunners. For – having created something out of the human spirit that did not exist before, he dedicates to the world of our century a vision that will remain among the most essential bequests of future generations. This modern-day poet of notable accomplishments enunciates the same venerable appeal to the collected wisdom of humanity, as the American writer, William Faulkner (1897-1962) articulated in his acceptance speech for the Nobel Prize in Literature in 1950:

I decline to accept the end of man. It is easy enough to say that man is immortal simply because he will endure: that when the last dingdong of doom has clanged and faded from the last worthless rock hanging tideless in the last red and dying evening, that even then there will still be one more sound: that of his puny inexhaustible voice, still talking. I refuse to accept this. I believe that man will not merely endure: he will prevail. He is immortal, not because he alone among creatures has an inexhaustible voice, but because he has a soul, a spirit capable of compassion and sacrifice and endurance. The poet's, the writer's duty is to write about these things. It is his privilege to help man endure by lifting his heart, by reminding him of the courage and honor and hope and pride and compassion and pity and sacrifice that have been the glory of his past. The poet's voice need not merely be the record of man, it can be one of the props, the pillars to help him endure and prevail.

Whether their lyrical compositions assume an emotion-filled or a neutral tone, the poets who have gathered to contribute to this extensive anthology are kindred spirits with those of whom Faulkner speaks. Their united voice rises through the hope to serve as "one of the props, the pillars to help [humanity] endure and prevail." Their commitment also expands to an invitation for the dissemination of the wisdom behind a warning label that the British poet and critic, Lascelles Abercrombie (1881-1938) left etched in his poem "The Box":

Once upon a time in the land of Hush-a-bye
Around about the wondrous days of yore
They came across a sort of box
Bound up with chains and locked with locks
And labeled, "Kindly Do Not Touch - It's War."

Decree was issued round about
All with a flourish and a shout
And a gaily colored mascot tripping lightly on before
"Don't fiddle with this deadly box
Or break the chains or pick the locks
And please don't ever play about with war."

Well the children understood
Children happen to be good
And they were just as good around the time of yore
They didn't try to pick the locks
Or break into that deadly box
They never tried to play about with war.

Mommies didn't either
Sisters, Aunts, or Grannies neither
Cause' they were quiet and sweet and pretty
In those wondrous days of yore.

Well, very much the same as now
Not the ones to blame somehow
For opening up that deadly box of war.
But someone did
Someone battered in the lid
And spilled the insides out across the floor.

A sort of bouncy bumpy ball
Made up of flags and guns and all
The tears and horror and death
That goes with war.

It bounced right out
And went bashing all about
And bumping into every thing in store.
And what was sad and most unfair
Is that it really didn't seem to care
Much who it bumped or why, or what, or for.

It bumped the children mainly
And I'll tell you this quite plainly
It bumps them everyday
And more and more.
And leaves them dead and burned and dying
Thousands of them sick and crying
Cause' when it bumps it's really very sore.

Now there's a way to stop the ball
It isn't difficult at all
All it takes is wisdom
And I'm absolutely sure
That we could get it back into the box
And bind the chains and lock the locks
But no one seems to want to save the children anymore.

Well, that's the way it all appears
Cause' it's been bouncing round for years and years
In spite of all that wisdom wiz'
Since those wondrous days of yore…
In the time they came upon a box
Bound up with chains and locked with locks
And labeled, "Kindly Do Not Touch - It's War"

In unison, the architect and the contributors of *World Healing World Peace 2014, a Poetry Anthology* join the Greek poet Theocritus (315 BC-260 BC) in his foreseeing love for humanity – the essence of enduring strength to permeate any disruption and decline in any world society:

And may all our towns spoiled by enemy hands
be peopled by their former citizens
again. May they work the fertile fields,
and may countless thousands of sheep fatten
in pastures and go bleating over the plain,
and may cattle coming home in herds
warn the late traveler to hurry
on his way. And may the fallow ground
be plowed at seed-time when the cicada
sings overhead in the treetops, watching
the shepherds in the sun. And may spiders
spin their slender webs over battle-weapons,
and the battle-cry be heard no more.

Idylls: From Number 16

hülya n. yilmaz

~ * ~

Dr. Hulya Yilmaz is a Senior Lecturer at Penn State University. She teaches German, Turkish and Comparative Literature. She is also an available Free Lance Writer, Editor, Literary Translator and Professional Book Reviewer.

for more information, Dr. Yilmaz may be contacted via : hnu1@psu.edu

Dr. hülya yılmaz is a college professor in Liberal Arts with an extensive teaching career. She authored a research book on the influence of ghazal poetry by Rumi and Hafız on 19th and 20th century German literature. Another scholarly work contains her chapter on a controversial novel by Orhan Pamuk, the 2006 recipient of the Nobel Prize for Literature. From her profession, however, she cherishes most the conduct and words of appreciation from a respectable number of students. In her creative work, yılmaz prefers the genres of fictional autobiography, short story and poetry. Presently, she teaches full-time in her fields of specialty; does creative writing; is a self-appointed literary translator and a novice free-lance writer.

www.worldhealingworldpeacepoetry.com

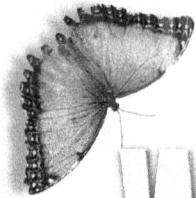

a few words from … **Dr. Peter C. Rogers**

Clearly, we are living in a time when we are starting to realize that we must work out our own salvation and that no one can do this for us. The road to peace leads to a journey that takes place on the inside which ultimately becomes our physical reality. We are living during a time where God is to be worshipped in spirit. These spiritual times are demanding much more of us in the way of personal introspection. If we are to achieve world peace or peace of any kind, we must first learn to live form our hearts. By living from the heart we will need to be guided by our own personal sense of spirituality and not some old worn out traditions. The spirituality I speak of cannot be taught. To try and teach someone what it is to be spiritual denies the very nature of spirituality because it is unique to each individual. There are many roads to enlightenment and if the road you're on has already been taken, chances are you're on the wrong path.

Each person must find for themselves what it is they have come here for not only in this lifetime but as a conscious being caught up on the wheel of reincarnation and repeated lifecycles. No matter how many times you deny the truth, it's still the truth. Truth is everlasting. There is great freedom in spirituality. Once we are able to shun the age old lies that have been imposed upon us by those living in fear seeking only to control the masses, we will then be able to step out of the darkness and into the marvelous light. This light is the pure essence of God in its entire splendor, God in the truest sense and not diluted by religion or dogma. Once we make the shift from the ideas that have been deeply ingrained in our consciousness by outdated traditions and generations of misinformation, we will have gained liberty from a spiritual tyranny that has long since been imposed upon Humanity. We will begin to seek out the truth for ourselves no longer falling for whatever someone offers us. We will question the status quo and become agitated by things being the way they are. Once this shift occurs, our realities will change and we will finally see the Matrix which is our life for all that it is, nothing more than a mere delusion. Our eyes will be opened and truth will reign supreme because the light of truth will be shed upon falsehood and the dark will no longer be able to exist in the light.

We must each come into our own awareness of peace with each gradual nudge of our spirit. Every occurrence, every lesson and every awakening will slowly beckon us into this full reality. My journey may not be the same as yours but I know for certain that there are many paths and only one summit, I'll meet you there.

Gaia is the planetary consciousness of every living creature that abides on it. It is a Universal phenomenon of creation that took place over billions of years ago. There will never be another Earth and science has yet to find a similar planet that can sustain life. Unfortunately, as a result of countless contributing factors, our planet is dying. We are depleting her in rapid proportions and sooner or later, she will die. When and how soon remains to be seen nevertheless at the rate we're headed, it will most certainly be a premature death. In order to prevent this untimely death, we must all learn to adhere to a higher sense of being. As such we will each need to adhere to a higher sense of being that coincides with elementary and universal truths that support all life.

Peter C. Rogers, D.D., Ph.D.

Dr. Peter C. Rogers, D.D., Ph.D., is a Light-Worker, a Life Coach, Motivational Speaker, Minister of Metaphysics and Spiritual Counselor.

He is the author of ***Ultimate Truth : Book I***, ***Universal Truth: Thinking Outside the Box : Book II*** and the up and coming ***One Hundred Disciplines to Higher Consciousness : A Conclusive Synopsis on Spiritual Principles***.

Dr. Rogers is a skilled lecturer and teacher of the Master Key System. He teaches an extensive class and has appeared on several shows to present this ancient system of manifestation formulated by Charles F. Haanel over 100 years ago. In 2010, Dr. Rogers founded a spiritual counseling practice called **TRUTH Dynamics** to help assist people in their quest for self realization.

Currently, he serves as the president of a Non-Profit organization called P.E.L.S.A which he and his wife formed in 2006 to assist people in overcoming addiction.

Dr. Rogers has been a student of Spirituality and Metaphysics for the past 20 years and in 2009, he received a Doctorate of Divinity in Spiritual Counseling as well as a Doctorate of Philosophy in Metaphysics from The University of Metaphysical Sciences. He currently resides in Long Beach, California where he continues to devote his time and energy writing, lecturing and mentoring others on their spiritual journey towards higher consciousness.

Peace
Quotes

We, Veteran's for Peace, view peace as a positively active and creative process which requires courage, commitment, endurance, vigilance, and integrity. Peace is a struggle toward unity, and it is characterized by an absence of violence in all its forms, including discrimination based on gender, age, race, religion, social and economic status, ethnicity, and sexual orientation. Those who labor for peace are called peacemakers because they tirelessly pursue nonviolent solutions, work for economic and social justice, celebrate diversity, and strive to build relationships between adversaries through education, conflict mediation, and humanitarian relief. We recognize that peace is both a means and end simultaneously, and that it is never finally or fully achieved. This is because change and growth require some degree of tension or conflict. Historically, such conflict has provided the impetus for military solutions. Thus we, Veteran's for Peace, strongly believe that the greatest obstacle to peace is militarism with its reliance on violence and war. We further believe that peacekeeping action should only be accomplished by a legitimate international body.

Committee to Define Peace, Veterans for Peace

You can't separate peace from freedom because no one can be at peace unless he has his freedom

Malcolm X

Peace is always beautiful.

Walt Whitman

Since wars begin in the minds of men, it is in the minds of men that the defenses of peace must be constructed.

UNESCO Constitution

Time itself becomes subordinate to war. If only we could celebrate peace as our various ancestors celebrated war; if only we could glorify peace as those before us, thirsting for adventure, glorified war; if only our sages and scholars together could resolve to infuse peace with the same energy and inspiration that others have put into war.

Why is war such an easy option? Why does peace remain such an elusive goal? We know statesmen skilled at waging war, but where are those dedicated enough to humanity to find a way to avoid war. Every nation has its prestigious military academies - or so few of them - that reach not only the virtues of peace but also the art of attaining it. I mean attaining and protecting it by means other than weapons, the tools of war. Why are we surprised whenever war recedes and yields to peace?

Elie Wiesel

If we have no peace, it is because we have forgotten that we belong to each other.

All works of love are works of peace.
I was once asked why I don't participate in anti-war demonstrations. I said that I will never do that, but as soon as you have a pro-peace rally, I'll be there.

Mother Theresa

The word *liberal* comes from the word *free*. We must cherish and honor the word *free* or it will cease to apply to us.
It isn't enough to talk about peace. One must believe in it. And it isn't enough to believe in it. One must work at it.

Elenor Roosevelt

World Healing ~ World Peace
Tee Shirts & Baseball Caps
Now Available

just $ 20.00 each
www.worldhealingworldpeacepoetry.com

all proceeds used to distribute Books to the United Nations & U.S. Congress

just $ 40.00 each
www.worldhealingworldpeacepoetry.com

all proceeds used to distribute Books to the United Nations & U.S. Congress

I support World Healing World Peace

www.worldhealingworldpeacepoetry.com

just $ 20.00 each

www.worldhealingworldpeacepoetry.com

all proceeds used to distribute Books to the United Nations & U.S. Congress

just $ 25.00 each

all proceeds used to distribute Books to the United Nations & U.S. Congress

other significant Anthologies from . . .

inner child press, ltd.

www.innerchildpress.com

World Healing
World Peace

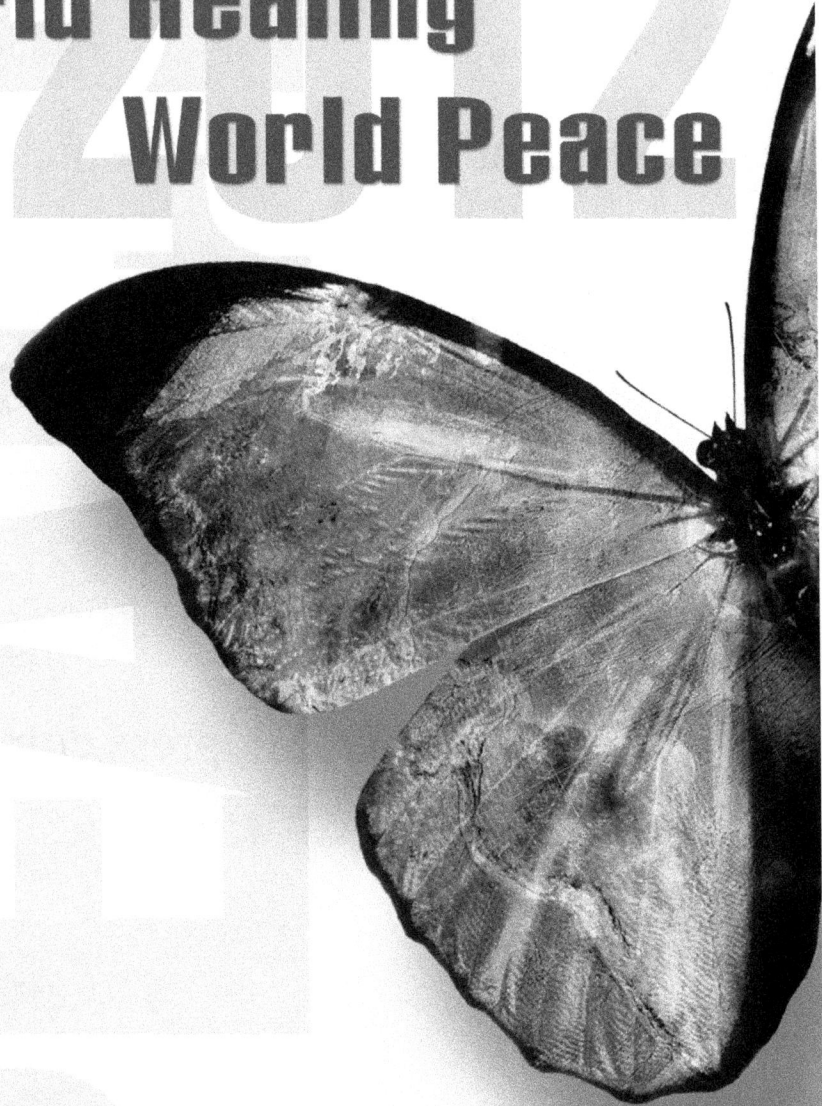

2012

A POETRY ANTHOLOGY
Volume 1

World Healing
World Peace

2012

A POETRY ANTHOLOGY
Volume 2

Mandela

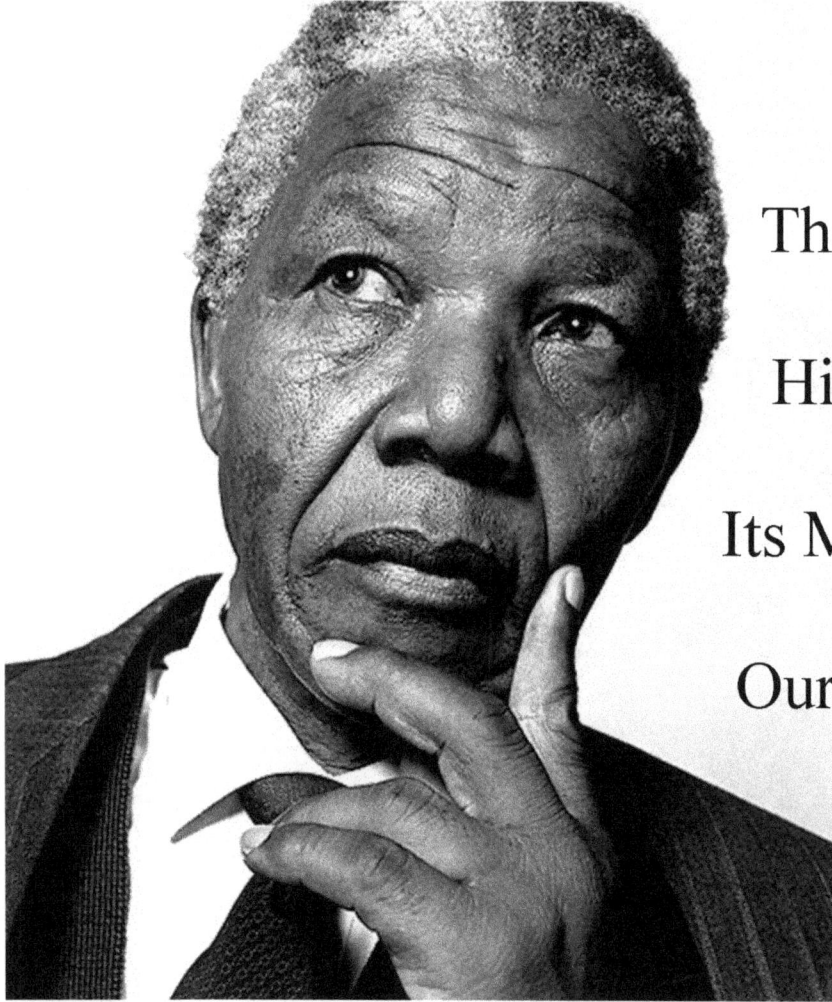

The Man

His Life

Its Meaning

Our Words

Poetry . . . Commentary & Stories
The Anthological Writers

A GATHERING OF WORDS

POETRY & COMMENTARY

FOR

TRAYVON MARTIN

healing through words

Poetry ... Prose ... Prayer ... Stories

PEOPLE OF EXTRAORDINARY TALENT

P.O.E.T.

ANTHOLOGY

FINDING YOUR VOICE
CLOSED MICS
DON'T GET FED

VOLUME 1

143

PEOPLE OF EXTRAORDINARY TALENT

P.O.E.T.

ANTHOLOGY

FINDING YOUR PURPOSE

A.C.T.I.O.N.

Artist
Coming
Together
In
Outstanding
Numbers

SPEAKS LOUDER THAN WORDS

VOLUME II

i

want my

PoEtRy

to . . .

a collection of the Voices of Many inspired by . . .

Monte Smith

a collection of the Voices of Many inspired by . . .

Monte Smith

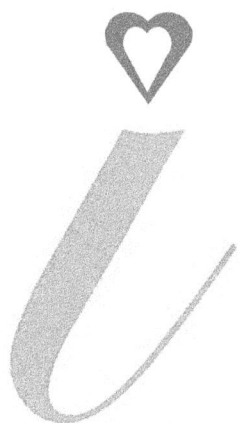
i

want my

PoEtRy

to . . .

volume II

PuZzled

...when the PIECES don't seem to fit.

Poets & Writers for Autism Awareness and Acceptance

Inner Child Press

Inner Child Press is a Publishing Company Founded and Operated by Writers. Our personal publishing experiences provides us an intimate understanding of the sometimes daunting challenges Writers, New and Seasoned may face in the Business of Publishing and Marketing their Creative "Written Work".

For more Information

Inner Child Press

www.innerchildpress.com

intouch@innerchildpress.com

www.ingramcontent.com/pod-product-compliance
Lightning Source LLC
Chambersburg PA
CBHW081229090426
42738CB00016B/3237